JOHN 14

The Most Important Chapter
In The New Testament

By

Allen C. Liles

JOHN 14

The Most Important Chapter In The New Testament

By

Allen C. Liles

Published By
Positive Imaging, LLC
9016 Palace Parkway
Austin, TX 78748
bill@positive-imaging.com

All Rights Reserved

No part of this publication may be reproduced in whole or in part, or stored in a retrieval system, or transmitted in any form or by any means, electronic, mechanical, printing, photocopying, recording or otherwise without written permission from the publisher, except for the inclusion of brief quotations in a review. For information regarding permission, contact the publisher.

Copyright   2020   Allen C. Liles

ISBN: 9781951776299

This book is dedicated to my dear wife
and partner in ministry Jan Carmen Liles

(1941-2017) RIP

Contents

Introduction	11
Preparation For Study Of John	15
John 14	19
Summary Of John 14 Key Points	23
Biblical Text And Commentary	27
A Tale Of Unexpected Loss	
John 14: 2-4	33
"I'll Come Back For You"	
John 14: 5-7	39
Angel Story	
John: 8-10	45
The Heroine's Journey	
John: 14-11	49
The Miracle	
John: 12-14	53
"Help Me Jesus"	
John 14: 15-17	59
"The Shy One	
John 14: 18-20	65
A Teacher's Legacy	

John 14: 21-22	**71**
The Forgotten Coach	
John: 14: 23-24	**77**
Helping Tremaine	
John:14: 25-26	**83**
The Daughter	
John:14: 27	**89**
Samantha's Talents	
John 14: 28-31	**95**
Bobby	
The Twelve Gifts Of John 14	**101**
The Gifts	
Conclusion	**111**
About The Author	**115**

"Do not let your hearts be troubled. You believe in God, believe also in me." *(John 14: 1)*

"Jesus answered, "I am the way and the truth and the life. No one comes to the father except through me." *(John 14:6)*

"Don't you believe that I am in the Father, and that the Father is in me?" *(John 14:10)*

"Believe me when I say that I am in the Father and the Father is in me, or believe on the evidence of the works themselves" *(John 14: 11)*

"Very truly I tell you, whoever believes in me will do the works I have been doing, and they will do even greater things than these." *(John 14:12)*

"And I will do whatever you ask in my name, so that the Father may be glorified in the son." *(John 14:13)*

"But the Advocate, the Holy Spirit, whom the Father will send in my name, will teach you all things." *(John 14:26)*

"Peace I leave with you, my peace I give you. I do not give as the world gives. Do not let your hearts be troubled and do not be afraid." *(John 14:27)*

INTRODUCTION

Introduction

There are many important chapters in the New Testament. Without question, the chapters in the gospels detailing Jesus' trial, crucifixion and resurrection are key in explaining the origin of Christianity. Yet, I believe there is one essential New Testament chapter for today's unique challenges. We are now living through a world changing pandemic, massive cultural shifts, an epidemic of loneliness, economic dislocation, civil unrest, political divisions, racial disharmony, addiction challenges and a spiritual separation from our Creator. Many of us feel confused, buffeted and alone as we face these relentless tests to our serenity.

I believe there is one specific chapter in the New Testament that could help us cope with our current problems. It offers a spiritual insight, wisdom and perspective that can provide clarity in an age of isolation and rampant negativity. The narrative contained in the 14th chapter of John occurs at a profound event in human history—The Last Supper. Jesus has brought His disciples together to hear some bad news. After three years of revolutionary teachings and startling miracles, their leader has informed them that He must leave. These loyal men, who had given up everything to follow Jesus, felt shocked and abandoned. The announcement of His imminent departure stunned and saddened them. What would happen now? Who could possibly replace the Master? Did they face imprisonment or even death because of their association with the Messiah? They needed an immediate explanation. Jesus understood their feelings of surprise and loss. He was also alarmed and worried. A trial and crucifixion would take place the following day. Jesus had gathered His closest followers together one final time to prepare them. What He shared at The Last Supper still reverberates today. As we walk our own human and spiritual Paths, fear and uncertainty surround us. We all need explanation and reassurance. We seek comfort and clarity in place of fear and confusion. I believe you and I can indeed find sustenance and hope in the prophetic words of Jesus. Whatever challenges you or I may be facing, we are never alone. The Holy Spirit lives within all of us. God is walking with each of us through the chaos. I hope this little book brightens your life and provides hope and understanding for both today and tomorrow.

Rev. Allen C. Liles

PREPARATION FOR STUDY OF JOHN 14

Opening Prayer before beginning consideration of John 14:
"God, please help me to become open and receptive to your Holy Word. Let me take the wisdom of John 14 into my heart and mind. I come to you now, humbly seeking the Way, the Truth and the Life. In Jesus name, I pray. Amen."

Meditation:
Find a quiet and comfortable place where you will not be disturbed for a minimum of 15 minutes. Sit with both feet flat on the floor. Put your hands in your lap with the palms turned upward. Now take a deep breath, breathing in through your nose. Hold your breath and count to five. Open your mouth and count to eight as you release your breath. Take one more deep breath and repeat the same process.

Now read these words: "God, please comfort and teach me. Come into my life. Guide and direct my steps. Allow me to feel your divine Presence and hear your sacred voice. I want to understand how the words of Jesus in John 14 can change my life for the better, starting today. Please activate the Holy Spirit within me now."

Close your eyes and sit in the silence for three to five minutes.
Open your eyes and repeat these words: "Thank you, thank you, thank you God. Amen." Now turn the page and read the 31 verses of John 14 at your normal speed. Do not try to consider in depth or reflect on any of the passages. Once you finish reading, close your eyes for at least 60 seconds and allow the sacred words of Jesus to penetrate your consciousness. You are now ready to proceed with a more detailed study of each verse, plus a collection of relevant spiritual stories.

JOHN 14
NIV

Verse 1—"Do not let your hearts be troubled. You believe in God, believe also in me.

2—My Father's house has many rooms; if that were not so, would I have told you that I am going there to prepare a place for you?

3—And if I go and prepare a place for you, I will come back and take you to be with me that you may also be where I am.

4—You know the way to the place I am going."

5—Thomas said to him, "Lord, we don't know where you are going, so how can we know the way?"

6—Jesus answered, "I am the way, and the truth and the life. No one comes to the Father except through me.

7—If you really know me, you will know my Father as well. From now on, you do know him and have seen him."

8—Philip said "Lord, show us the Father and that will be enough for us."

9—Jesus answered, "Don't you know me, Philip, even after I have been among you for such a long time? Anyone who has seen me has seen the Father. How can you say "Show us the Father"?

10—Don't you believe that I am in the Father and the Father is in me? The words I say to you I do not speak on my own authority. Rather, it is the Father living in me who is doing the work.

11—Believe me when I say that I am in the Father and the Father is in me; or at least believe on the evidence of the works themselves.

12—Very truly I tell you whoever believes in me will do the works I have been doing, and they will do even greater things than these because I am going to the Father.

13—And I will do whatever you ask in my name, so that the Father may be glorified in the son.

14—You may ask for anything in my name, and I will do it.

15—If you love me, keep my commands.

16—And I will ask the Father, and he will give you another advocate to help you and be with you forever—

17—the Spirit of truth. The world cannot accept him because it neither sees him nor knows him. But you know him, for he lives with you and will be in you.

18—I will not leave you as orphans; I will come to you.

19—Before long, the world will not see me anymore, but you will see me. Because I live, you will also live.

20—On that day, you will realize that I am in my Father, and you are in me and I am in you.

21—Whosoever has my commands and keeps them is the one who loves me. The one who loves me will be loved by my Father, and I too will love them and show myself to them.

22—Then Judas (not Judas Iscariot) said, "But Lord, why do you intend to show yourself to us and not the world?"

23—Jesus replied, "Anyone who loves me will obey my teaching. My Father will love them, and we will come to them and make our home with them.

24—Anyone who does not love me will not obey my teaching. These words you hear are not my own; they belong to the Father who sent me.

25—All this I have spoken while still with you.

26—But the Advocate, the Holy Spirit, whom the Father will send in My name, will teach you all things and will remind you of everything I have said to you.

27—Peace I leave with you; my peace I give you. I do not give as the world gives. Do not let your hearts be troubled and do not be afraid.

28—You heard me say, 'I am going away and am coming back to you.' If you loved me, you would be glad that I am going to the Father, for the Father is greater than I.

29—I have told you now before it happens, so that when it does happen you will believe.

30—I will not say much more to you, for the prince of the world is coming. He has no hold over me,

31—but he comes so that the world may learn that I love the Father and do exactly what my Father has commanded me. Come now. Let us leave."

SUMMARY OF JOHN 14 KEY POINTS

Summary Of John 14 Key Points

(1) Jesus informs the Disciples of his imminent departure from the physical world and comforts them.

(2) Jesus promises to return, gather up the Disciples and take them to Heaven where everyone can be together again in rooms that He has specially prepared.

(3) Jesus explains his Oneness with God by telling them "I am in the Father and the Father is in me."

(4) He tells them that if they believe, they can also do the "Greater Works".

(5) Jesus unveils the concept and arrival of his replacement, The Holy Spirit.

(6) Jesus reiterates the principle of Oneness, that he is in the Father and the Father is in him.

(7) He promises that the Holy Spirit will "teach them in all things".

(8) Jesus explains that the peace he leaves will exceed that of what the world can deliver.

(9) He focuses on the need for the Disciples to keep His commands and to obey God.

(10) Jesus reassures His closest followers they will not be left alone after his departure.

(11) He stipulates that if the Disciples love him, they will carry His teachings forward after he departs.

(12) His entire message in John 14 is one of explanation, instruction, comfort, and hope.

Author of the Book of John: The Apostle John: "The Disciple that Jesus Loved."

Date of authorship: 90-100 A. D.

Occasion where event took place: "The Last Supper" or "Lord's Supper", one day before Jesus' trial and crucifixion. Now observed in Christian tradition as Maundy Thursday, the day before Good Friday. It was celebrated then on the first day of Passover or the Festival of the Unleavened Bread.

Probable Location: "The Upper Room" on Mount Zion, just outside the walls of the Old City of Jerusalem.

In attendance: Jesus and His Disciples: Peter, Andrew, James, son of Alphaeus, John, Matthew, Philip, Thomas, Bartholomew, James, son of Zebedee, Judas, Jude, and Simon. In Leonardo da Vinci's late 1490s mural "The Last Supper", the figure to Jesus' left is said to resemble Mary Magdalene. Some accounts insist that at least fifteen people attended the meal, including several who assisted in preparing the food. Others contend that Judas did not attend the full meal.

Other facts: The Last Supper provides the scriptural basis for the Eucharist, also known as Holy Communion.

BIBLICAL TEXT AND COMMENTARY

JOHN 14: 1--"Do not let your hearts be troubled. You believe in God. Believe in me also."

No human relationship is permanent. Change and loss come to everyone. Losses occur regularly in every life. When you lose someone or something important, life shifts. Adjustments must be made, whether you are prepared or not. New patterns are bound to emerge. Nothing can ever be taken for granted.

We are all subject to the sudden fear and anxiety caused by changing circumstances. Losing a loved one creates special stress. This even includes loss of a beloved pet. Experiencing the physical departure of a spouse, significant other, a parent, a child, or a friend can leave anybody feeling lost and adrift. Departing from a longtime place of employment also can produce sadness and consternation. Being separated from the familiar can throw anyone into a tailspin.

As we stumble through our new physical and emotional realities, comfort and support become our primary needs. Many of us have family, friends, a church, various support groups or trained professionals available to help with the grief process. But many others must navigate the uncertainties of loss alone or with minimum help. We are told that time heals everything, but sometimes the hands of a clock move slowly or not at all.

In John 14, Jesus has shocked the Disciples by announcing his imminent departure. Remember that only a few days earlier, both they and Jesus had received a triumphant welcome into Jerusalem. Flowers and palm leaves were strewn in their path. Now, without warning, the Master was leaving them. In modern day terms, it might be comparable to a head coach winning the Super Bowl game on Sunday and then leaving town on Monday. These most dedicated followers of Jesus felt blindsided and abandoned. Who could blame them? In addition, the various explanations of his actions seemed murky and mysterious. Who is this invisible creature known as the Holy Spirit?

How could something unseen ever take the place of the Messiah? What would happen to them? Arrest? Trial and possible imprisonment or even worse? Jesus understood their hard questions and scattered feelings. In John 14:1, He sought to comfort and reassure them. He also invoked the name of God, the Higher Power, in helping guide them through the upset. Jesus acknowledged their belief in both Him and God. When sudden change confronts us, it is normal to feel scattered, confused and alone. We want and need something or someone to lead us through the deep valleys of grief and loss. Human beings today are no different.

A Tale Of Unexpected Loss:

Charles and Linda, both in their early 70s, were enjoying the Golden Years. Both were retired. Charles had been a pulpit minister at the same church for 25 years. Linda had served alongside her husband as the head bookkeeper at the church. Working together in a religious setting had been an incredible blessing and fulfilling experience. The first years of their retirement did not require any major adjustment as the pair was accustomed to being together 24/7. They had one daughter, 45-year old Charlene, who had lived on the opposite coast for many years. In-person visits with their only child were infrequent. Char was a nursing supervisor at a major hospital and always seemed busy with her job. She was married briefly to a fellow nurse from another country. That marriage had ended nearly two decades ago and produced no grandchildren. Charles and Linda usually texted their daughter on her birthday and at Christmas. It had been nearly three years since they last spoke on the phone. The couple wanted to fly out for a visit after retiring from the church, but Charlene discouraged it. The subject was not broached again. None of Char's childhood or school friends ever called to inquire about her. For all practical purposes, their daughter had vanished. Still, Charles and Linda had each other. The feeling of being estranged from their only child did not detract from their overall happiness. Charles and Linda knew their daughter had a roommate named Kristin. She was an executive with a large tech company. One day, a wedding announcement arrived unexpectedly in the mail. Charlene and Kristin had gotten married in a civil ceremony. Charles and Linda were not only surprised. They felt blindsided and hurt. Charlene had not only excluded them. She had specifically chosen not to be married in a church setting. It felt like a disrespectful slap in their face. That Char had opted for a same sex marriage did not trouble them. But having everything sprung on them without warning felt unfair and jarring. Charles felt shortchanged that he had not been there to give his daughter away. Officiating at the service also would have been a pleasant duty. However, he and Linda put aside their surprise and disappointment. They texted Charlene and Kristin their congratulations and asked if a telephone or Skype visit might be possible. Charlene texted back that she and Kristin were on their way to the airport for a honeymoon flight to Tokyo. "By the way," she added, "We're both planning to move there next month." Charles and Linda were now openly reeling from the suddenness of everything. That night, Linda began experiencing chest pains. Charles had immediately called 911. By the time paramedics and police arrived, she was already gone. He later sat dumbfounded in his living room chair, side by side to his wife's now empty chair. The next few weeks were emotionally numbing for the ex-pastor. Linda's funeral at the church had been an elaborate event, attended by hundreds. Their daughter was not present. She did call from Tokyo to offer condolences and an apology for not being there in person. Charles was comforted and overwhelmed by the support and empathy of his former congregants. However, for many who face the grieving process, outside concern and interest tend to ebb over time. About six months after Linda passed, Charles found himself feeling alone and depressed. When they were together in marriage and work, he had never once imagined or contemplated life without her. They had never discussed the subject of one losing the other. He felt totally lost and unprepared for widowerhood. He prayed every day for divine guidance and direction, but God seemed strangely quiet. Charles had reached out twice to his daughter since Linda passed, but their conversations seemed remote and perfunctory. They did not discuss getting together in person. One morning, as he sat in meditation, Charles asked God for a specific favor. Could Linda's Spirit return for one final conversation? He had often sat in his solitary chair and talked to her. However, he had never sensed her conversing back with him. Without warning, he suddenly felt his dear wife's presence. Then, her words sprang from somewhere deep within the core of his being. He heard: "First of all, my darling, I'm fine. Heaven is a wonderful environment in which to spend eternity. I am looking forward to you joining me here. I have been preparing a beautiful place for us. It is quite lovely and comfortable. I think you will like it. I know you feel alone and lost without me. Please know that I am never that far away from you. I am keeping a close watch on how you are doing. Try to release any expectations about Charlene. She is traveling her own spiritual and human path. Just wish her safe travels on the journey. I have come today to reassure you. You still have more work to do for God. A church near you is searching for an interim minister. Do not worry, my dearest, they will find you soon. When you deliver that first sermon in the new church, I will be there in the front row cheering you on. Believe what I tell you, my sweet husband: God and I will never leave or forsake you. Trust us. You are never alone." From that moment, Charles' feelings of abandonment and loss lessened considerably. By connecting with God and his dear departed wife, the world had brightened forever.

JOHN 14: 2-4

JOHN 14:2—"My Father's House has many rooms; if that were not so, would I have told you that I am going there to prepare a place for you?

JOHN 14:3—And if I go to prepare a place for you, I will come back and take you with me that you also may be where I am.

JOHN 14: 4—You know the way to the place where I am going."

John 14: 2-4

In these three verses, Jesus again seeks to reassure his followers. He provides a description of God's Kingdom to which the Disciples can somewhat relate. Heaven is a "big" place, large enough to offer enough rooms for everybody. No one will be left outside the walls, abandoned and homeless. Saying that he was "going to prepare a place for you" also suggests a specific reason for his unexpected departure. Perhaps only Jesus can handle the preparation. He also assures the Disciples of his eventual return. He will personally come back and fetch them for the trip. That means Jesus plans to act as their spiritual escort to Heaven. They will not be required to make the eternal journey alone. However, his reminder that they "know the way to the place where I am going" probably confused the Disciples. Jesus had never sat down with them and discussed any of the specific details. Perhaps he felt their trust in God and him meant they inherently understood the concept of Heaven and eternity. The Master had to be aware of the shock and dismay that would accompany his departure.

"I'll Come Back for You":

Margaret fell in love with Jason when she was in the second grade. He was a big-time fourth grader and the tallest boy in his class. She tried with no success to get his attention. They were together again in middle school, but only for one year. He played every sport and was always busy with practice or games. Margaret did see him around the campus occasionally with one of the school cheerleaders. There were rumors the pair might be "going steady". Margaret caught up to Jason again when she entered the ninth grade. By this time, her figure had filled out. She started getting teased about the enormous size of her breasts from both sexes. By that time, Jason had settled on basketball as his primary sport. He was already six-five and still growing. College scouts were attending his games. One day, when Margaret was walking down the main hall in high school, Jason came around a corner and literally ran over her. She lay sprawled on the floor looking up at this young giant. The love from second grade returned full force. He apologized, gently helped her up, and asked if she was O. K. The high school junior also gaped at her uncommon God-given endowments. She got his attention this time. Soon, Jason began walking her to a few classes. Then he started offering her rides home from school on occasion. Margaret's parents were not too thrilled about the attention, but her dad was a basketball fan and that counted for a lot. They did not have sex for more than a year. However, the couple celebrated Margaret's 16th birthday by making love in the back seat of his car. Two months later, Margaret was pregnant. Consternation and accusations followed with both sets of parents. Jason's mom and dad worried about the end of any college sports scholarship and even a possible NBA career for their talented son. Margaret's parents just felt ashamed and guilty about not doing a better job in raising their child. Their daughter never mentioned that she had loved Jason since elementary school. A mutual decision was made by everyone to have the child and then place it in the adoption process. Margaret dropped out of school and was sent to live with a divorced aunt in another state. A midwife helped deliver a healthy baby daughter at the aunt's home. Margaret surrendered the baby to a local placement agency and then returned for her senior year. By that time, Jason had graduated from high school and was enrolled at a Division I university on a basketball scholarship. Before he left town, he had written Margaret a letter. "I'm leaving now," he told her, "but I'll come back for you some day. I promise. I'm going to prepare a life for us." But it did not happen. Jason went on to the NBA for a moderately successful eight-year career. Margaret later learned he had married one of the team's cheerleaders. Meanwhile, she earned a nursing degree at the local campus of a major university. Time passed. Margaret dated several men, but none seemed to compare with her one true love. Then *without warning, Jason contacted her unexpectedly. It had been 10 years since they last spoke. He was divorced now after a brief marriage. He asked if they might keep in touch via Skype and the internet. She said yes because her feelings for him had never died. A few months later, he decided to move back to his hometown and pursue their relationship in person. Eighteen months after Jason returned, he and Margaret stood at the altar of a local church pledging their vows. The officiant of their wedding was a new interim minister at the church named "Charles". He was a nice man who had been widowed for a year or so. "I told Margaret I would come back for her," Jason told the minister, "And I guess God held me to my word. Thank you, God."*

JOHN 14: 5-7

JOHN 14: 5—Thomas said to him, "Lord, we don't know where you are going, so how can we know the way?"

JOHN 14:6—Jesus answered, "I am the way, the truth and the life. No one comes to the Father except through me.

JOHN 14:7—If you really know me, you will know my Father as well. From now on, you do know him and have seen him."

John 14: 5-7

The Disciples were having problems understanding what Jesus was telling them. They had only a general idea of where the Master was going, except to a large place with rooms enough to accommodate them. At least he was promising to come back for them. That helped because they had no specific directions on how to get there on their own. Jesus was assuring them: "I am the way, the truth and the life." He also added: "No one comes to the Father except through me." Therefore, by remaining faithful, they could reasonably assume he would come back and show them "the way." The "truth" Jesus talked about evidently referred to his teachings and precepts. Adding "the life" to his statement more than likely meant "the saved" or spiritual life. However, it also seemed clear that the Master was making a broad statement that included everyone who chose to follow him. In the following verse, Jesus linked himself directly to God. He reminded the Disciples of his close relationship with the Father, again reassuring them of his own divinity. Jesus' oneness with God, the ultimate Father, reflected a key element of his holiness. The fact that Thomas sought clarification from Jesus about "knowing the way" shows how comfortable they must have been questioning their leader. In response, the Messiah was seeking the Disciples' complete trust and understanding as the unexpected situation played itself out. One can feel the chaos and uncertainty that was gripping everyone.

Angel Story:

Papa was dying. His family knew the old man's death was imminent. He had just celebrated his 90th birthday. Papa had whispered to his son Paul "I want to make it until 90. Then I'm done." Papa and Paul shared the same birthday. Paul himself had just turned 65, another milestone. The pair made plans to spend their two special birthdays together with some quality alone time. However, a week before the birthdays, Papa had been whisked to the hospital with chest pains. He was being kept in the Cardiac Care

Unit for tests and observation. So, the birthday reunion was rescheduled for the elder man's hospital room. He had given strict instructions to Margaret, his CCU nurse, that his son should be given priority. "Now I know you just got married to your old boyfriend. What's name? Jason?" he chided Margaret, "But keep everybody else out while my son is here." She promised to do so. As Paul sat facing his father, he detected some obvious sadness. "What's wrong, Papa? he asked. "I really am leaving soon," the old man answered, "I won't be coming home from the hospital." Paul tried to ease the conversation by smiling and saying, "Don't say that! Of course, you are coming home." "No," Papa insisted, "Just listen to me. Before I go, I need to get some things off my chest. Since Mama died, you are the only one who really understands me. So, move a little closer and listen up. I don't the strength to repeat myself." Paul pulled his chair closer and leaned forward. He felt honored that Papa trusted him enough to share his closest secrets. "What is it, Papa?" Paul asked. His father grinned for the first time and said "I want you give some hand-me-down history about the family You knew that your grandpa, my father, was once a sheriff back in Texas and before we moved here?" "Yes," Paul answered, "He never talked much about it." Well, there was a reason for that," the old man said. "I am going to share it with you now. He was a deputy sheriff in a county on the Red River, the border between Texas and Oklahoma. Your grandpa was a young man for a job like that, only in his late 20s. However, there was something very extraordinary about him." "What was that Papa?" Paul asked. "He was the only black deputy sheriff in the entire state of Texas at the time," the old man smiled. "Daddy was very light-skin and he was often mistaken for being white. Your great-grandfather was the town doctor for the black community and knew the regular sheriff very well. He convinced the guy to put my father on as a deputy-in-training. They couldn't tell anyone that he was an actual sheriff or the white folks would have

John 14: 5-7

rebelled. Most all of Daddy's policing was in the black community. That worked out for everybody and the regular sheriff was pleased with him. But one day all hell broke loose. A young man in the community was accused of trying to kiss a white woman. Daddy knew that just the opposite had happened, but the woman got scared and accused the man of pressuring her. Anyway, they threw the boy in jail at the County Courthouse on a Friday night. It just so happened that the regular sheriff was whitetail dove hunting down in the Rio Grande Valley and the #1 deputy's wife was having a baby. So, my father was the only officer on duty when the mob showed up Saturday night with a rope. Daddy barred the doors, but he honestly did not know what might happen if they broke in and found TWO black boys inside the jail. "What on earth did he do?" Paul inquired. "All of a sudden," Papa said, "A tall man in a big white hat came barreling through the crowd and walked toward the Courthouse. "Who are you?" somebody in the mob yelled. The big man called out, "I'm Texas Ranger Paul Walker. Now get the hell out of my way before I shoot your ass off." Daddy heard the commotion and he quickly opened the door for Ranger Walker. He tall man came swooping in and said, "I heard you were having a riot over here and they sent me to see if you needed any help." "I'm glad you're here," my daddy said, "But you're just one Ranger." The man just gave him a steely-eyed look and said "Well, there is only one riot." That legend has been passed down for over a century. And my daddy was the first one that heard it. Anyway, a couple of years before the family headed north, Daddy tried to find that Ranger and thank him again. That is when he discovered something strange." "What is that?" his son asked. "The Texas Rangers had no record of anyone named Paul Walker ever working for them. Somebody must have sent an angel down from Heaven that night to rescue my Daddy and the other boy. That young man later went free when the woman changed her story. Anyway, that is why we named you Paul. It is also why you probably decided *to become a law enforcement officer. Your namesake is a full-fledged angel who also carried a badge. Never forget it! I am looking forward to shaking that angel's hand in a few days. When you get up to Heaven someday, I'll introduce you." Then, Papa closed his eyes and whispered, "You go on now. Promise me that someday you will share that story with my grandson Paul, Jr. You will do that for me, won't you? "Yes, Papa," Paul said, "Absolutely! It will be my honor."*

JOHN 8-10

JOHN 14:8—Philip said "Lord, show us the Father and that will be enough for us."

JOHN 14:9—Jesus answered, "Don't you know me, Philip, even after I have been among you for such a long time? Anyone who has seen me has seen the Father. How can you say, "Show us the Father"?

JOHN 14:10—Don't you believe that I am in the Father and the Father is in me? The words I say to you I do not speak on my own authority. Rather, it is the Father living in me who is doing the work."

In this passage, Jesus seems almost frustrated that the Disciples still do not grasp some of his basic spiritual principles. But you can almost understand their human uncertainties about their leader. His trusted followers look at The Master through mortal eyes. In doing so, they perceive a man just like them. Yet, when Jesus performs uncommon miracles and speaks wisdom beyond their comprehension, he takes on the guise of a God from some distant universe. Jesus sees this paradox and tries to address it. He is explaining that an inner or Higher Power is the real Source of his otherworldly abilities. He presents God and himself as interchangeable. Perhaps this is asking too much from the Disciples. Remember, they knew Jesus before God endowed their friend with divine capabilities. In many of their minds, he was still the Jesus of humble origin—a carpenter's son. It must be a stretch for them to understand what he means by the statement "I am in the Father and the Father is in me." Yet, this is the essence of pure spiritualty When God created us, He placed a spark of divinity at our core: the soul.

The Heroine's Journey:

Six-year old Maria had to grow up fast. Her mother Gabriella was only 16 when she gave birth to the dark-haired baby. Maria never knew her father. Juan had left Matamoras for Mexico City before her first birthday. Gabriella and Maria never heard from him again. "Just as well," her mother told her. They were fortunate that Gabriella's parents loved them both unconditionally and provided a home for them. However, money and jobs were scare in this city in the north of Mexico. One day the family decided to take their chances going across the border at Reynosa, across from McAllen, Texas. Maria's father Jose had some good contacts, paid a modest fee and their night-time crossing went smoothly. An old bus was waiting to transport them and a dozen others all the way to Corpus Christi, more than 150 miles away. The bus had broken down a couple of times, but still made the trip before dawn came up on the Gulf Coast. The four immigrants, or "illegals" as the Texans called them, found immediate refuge with one of Gabriella's cousins and her husband. The accommodations were sparse, but similar to what they had experienced in Matamoras. However, Texas was getting tough and beginning to round up people who had crossed the border without approval. One day Jose announced they were heading north to another state. It took several weeks and some delays, but they finally made it. Things went better than expected. Maria was able to start the first grade in a nearby elementary school. Gabriella found work as a waitress at a pancake house. Meanwhile her mother and father located jobs as a domestic and a gardener, respectively, for a well-to-do black family. The lady of the house was a physician and the husband served in law enforcement. They had one son, Paul, Jr. One day, when Gabriella had a day off from the pancake house, she went with her mother to assist in cleaning the employer's house. Gabriella wore a bright yellow sun dress that day. She also had placed a flower in her hair, something she had never done before. Although the lady doctor was at the hospital and the police officer dad was at the station, Paul, Jr. was seated at the kitchen table studying for his school exams. When Gabriella was introduced to him, he commented on the bright flower in her hair. She blushed and thanked him with a shy "Gracias, senor". "Do you speak English?" he asked her. "Muy poco," the young Hispanic woman smiled. "Would you like to learn?" Paul, Jr. asked. "Yes, sir" she had answered in perfect English. Their friendship began and blossomed. Four years later, Paul Jr. and Gabriella were married with both sets of parents beaming their approval. Maria, then 10 years old, was her mother's Maid of Honor.

JOHN 14:11

JOHN 14:11—Believe Me when I say that I am in the Father and the Father is in me; or believe on the evidence of the works themselves.

Being in Oneness with God was at the core of Jesus' message. He wanted the Disciples to understand his indivisible relationship with an imminent and transcendent Father. In this verse, Jesus was also saying: "Do you really think I could have performed those miracles without God's help?" Still, the concept of God and Jesus being interchangeable had to challenge the Disciples' logic. They were fishermen, tax collectors and everyday people. Believing in their leader's Oneness with God required radical thinking. Of course, they witnessed the incredible miracles and had heard Jesus speak the higher wisdom. Yet, accepting that the Master enjoyed a Oneness with God required an extra portion of faith and belief. No Disciple wanted to question the concept of Oneness, but Jesus must have felt their skeptical attitude. For them to go forward with Jesus' ministry after his departure, they needed to comprehend and believe what he was saying.

The Miracle:

Angela had been an ER doc for almost four years. She loved the immediacy of this aspect of medicine. No two days were ever alike. Some could be more routine than others, but dull moments were few and far between. She had seen some miraculous and unexplainable moments take place in the ER. But one stood out that changed her belief in miracles. It happened during a recent summer. Violent crime had suddenly spiked to its highest level in many years. Since her husband Paul was a police officer, she heard almost nightly horror stories. Gun violence, especially involving young people, seemed out of control. One night in the ER, Angela witnessed a wrenching episode. A little girl had, probably no more than five, been playing dolls in the living room of her mother's home. A stray bullet crashed through the window and struck the youngster. Paramedics and police were on the scene in less than eight minutes. During that time, the mother was crying and hysterical. Her daughter lay lifeless on the living room floor, pooled in blood. Suddenly, the little girl's mother witnessed her daughter hanging suspended on the ceiling, tethered by invisible ropes. Later at the hospital, she told Angela that the little girl distinctly said, "Don't worry, Mama, I'll be OK." She was rushed to the hospital. A paramedic radioed the hospital that he was bringing in a gunshot victim, but that the child involved "didn't make it." Still, they wheeled her quickly into the ER where Angela was the attending physician. As they hoisted the girl off the gurney and onto the operating table, Angela asked the location of the gunshot. "I don't really know," the EMS technician told Angela, "I assume somewhere in the chest or heart." They stripped the young child's clothing off. To everyone's amazement, there was no visible wound. Angela took the mother aside and asked for more details about what had happened. "I heard the gunshot and the glass shattering," the mother said, "I saw my baby lying on the floor with blood around her and I panicked". Then, she added the bit about seeing her daughter suspended on the ceiling for a few seconds and what she had said about being OK. Angela quickly checked the little girl's vitals. She had normal breathing and her blood pressure was fine. Frank, the EMT who brought her in was standing with his mouth open. "I swear she was dead when we got here," Frank said with some wonder. Then, he added, "I think I just witnessed a miracle." He then handed Dr. Angela the little girl's doll that he had swooped up for the ride to the hospital. It was a dark-haired black angel, clothed in a beautiful orchid dress. The angel was smiling.

JOHN 12-14

John 14: 12—Very truly I tell you, whosoever believes in me will do the works I have been doing and they will do even greater things than these, because I am going to the Father.

John 14: 13—And I will do whatever you ask in my name, so that my Father may be glorified in the son.

John 14:14—You may ask me for anything in my name, and I will do it."

Jesus knew the Disciples felt inadequate about equaling his miracle working and wisdom teaching. In truth, none of them felt capable of following his performance in any area. Since they did not fully understand or interpret what Jesus was saying, it would be unthinkable they could succeed him. Yet, here he was assuring them they could accomplish greater things than him. Who was he kidding? Raising people from the dead? Making the blind see? Walking on the water and calming the storm? And what about feeding the five thousand and still having food left over? No way, they thought. Yet, Jesus absolutely needed to instill confidence and faith in those he left behind. If they would only believe, he was promising them success. Jesus also wanted the Disciples to stay forever connected with him. Although his physical presence would not be around, he urged his followers to ask for help "in my name". He was then promising to respond and grant their request if it was framed as he directed. He made it a point by repeating this assurance in two consecutive verses # 12 and #13. Jesus wanted the Disciples to believe in themselves as worthy successors. But it would not be an easy sell.

"Help Me Jesus":

Frank had been an EMT for nearly eight years. It had not been an easy path. He first had to deal with some legal and financial problems, brought about by some bad personal choices. Frank had hooked up with a group of former high school buddies who were into selling marijuana and shoplifting. Pot had not yet been legalized in his home state, so Frank and his friends had become suppliers of choice for literally hundreds of people. However, a couple of their customers were narcs bent on keeping the weed trade as disorganized and local as possible. Being considered one of the ringleaders, Frank was arrested. He was given a one-year felony sentence commuted down to nine months. The authorities were hopeful that a few months behind bars might straighten Frank out. They were right. He dropped his wayward friends, totally quit drinking and using any type of drugs. He also graduated from a two-year community college with an Associates of Arts degree. In addition, Frank completed an EMT training course, finishing #1 in his class. The demand in his profession was high because of a world pandemic, so he was able to find a job. He had been promoted now a couple of times and his future looked good. His name had even been mentioned in a recent article in a major newspaper. He had transported a young girl, who everyone thought had been shot and killed, to the ER of a local hospital. It turned out there were no wounds in her body. Everyone pronounced it a miracle and indeed it was, at least on Frank's eyes. He was not a praying young man, but that night he thanked Jesus for sparing the girl's life. After the brief notoriety, things settled down for Frank. Then, about six weeks later, he popped into a Walmart store to pick up a few items before his regular shift. He was driving his Emergency Services vehicle, as he needed to be on official duty in about 30 minutes. Frank had been inside the store about five minutes when he heard several gunshots from the front. He quickly called 911 and alerted the operator about the situation. Other calls were also coming in. He peeked around the corner and saw two armed masked men going from cashier to cashier. They were robbing the cashiers at each register and placing the money in large trash bags. To Frank's knowledge, he had never heard of such a brazen robbery against a large store. Many of the stores had security officers now. Then, Frank saw a man on the floor and surmised he could have been store security. Frank's emergency training kicked in and he began edging closer to the front of the store. The victim obviously needed some professional help. It was then that a third robber entered the store. This person carried an AR-15 and began waving it toward customers in the check-out lanes. A full panic was now setting in. Although all three gunmen were wearing face masks, something about the man with the *automatic weapon seemed familiar. Looking closer, Frank recognized one of his close running buddies from the marijuana operation. Frank had been questioned about the person's involvement after his own arrest, but he had chosen not to "rat" him out. His buddy had "skated" and Frank later heard about his gratitude. Now, the former friend stood at the front of a major retail store with a dangerous weapon and lots of innocent people in harm's way. A thought came into Frank's mind: "Help me, Jesus. I'm asking for you to help me with this problem." Suddenly, he knew exactly what to do. He raised his hands high in the air and walked into plain view. "Stop!" he shouted directly to his former partner in crime. "I'm EMS. Let me help the injured guy! Do you really want a murder charge too?" The man with the AR-15 stopped and gazed intently at Frank. "Is that you?" he shouted, "What are you doing here?" "I'm trying to save your ass—again!" Frank answered, "For God's sake, try not to be an idiot! Do you want to go to jail for life!" One of the other robbers called out "Who the hell is this guy?". Frank's former partner in crime looked momentarily confused. Then, without warning, he screamed "Let's get the hell out of here now!". He waved the weapon at his companions and they all bolted for the door. In the store back office, the manager remotely locked the doors behind them. "Take cover now!" Frank yelled to the frightened customers. Everyone hunkered down as gunfire erupted in the parking lot between a police SWAT team and the three criminals. It was over in less than a minute. Later, the city police chief marveled that a hostage situation or mass casualties had not resulted from the incident. More than a few customers remarked about Frank's uncommon bravery. "I had some help," he told everyone, but did not elaborate. One reporter noted in her story that Frank was the same EMT who had witnessed the miracle in the ER. "Once again, he was in the right place at the right time," she wrote. "Somebody must be watching over him."*

JOHN 14: 15-17

JOHN 14: 15: "If you love me, keep my commands.

JOHN 14: 16: And I will ask the Father and He will give you another advocate to help you and be with you forever—

John 14: 17: The Spirit of Truth. The world cannot accept him, because it neither sees nor knows him. But you know him, for he lives with you and will be in you."

John 14: 15-17

In these key verses, Jesus makes the Disciples a somewhat conditional promise. If they love him, they will keep his teachings and commands after he departs. If they will follow this request, he promises to send a replacement in the form of "The Spirit of Truth." This represents The Holy Spirit, an unseen but powerful "Advocate". At this point, Jesus knows the Disciples require concrete assurance they will not be forgotten or forsaken. He also seeks to lock in their loyalty and willingness to continue his ministry. Jesus acknowledges that the material culture will not accept or believe in anything invisible. He is also introducing and reaffirming the concept that the Holy Spirit already lives within each one of them. Jesus understands that acceptance of an "Advocate" will require a tremendous leap of faith by his loyal followers. Replacing Jesus would not be easy, perhaps impossible.

"The Shy One":

Belinda had been shy since kindergarten. She was now 18 and a high school senior. Things had not improved much over the years. Although her looks were not the problem, Belinda had scored exactly four dates in the past four years. All were pure torture. Her shyness made for an awkward experience. She only spoke when asked a direct question and the response was usually one or two words. Belinda's mother had her daughter in therapy three times, including when she was seven years old. The doctors had all declared defeat after a few months. "There is really nothing wrong with her," one counselor told Belinda's mother, "She is just more comfortable not talking." Now, as graduation loomed, her parents were facing their biggest problem yet. Belinda was graduating with honors and wanted to attend college. Yet, her mom and dad worried about the social interactions required on the college level. To their knowledge, Belinda had never smoked a single joint and or taken a drink of alcohol. That did not prepare their daughter for college life in her parents slightly outdated opinion. Belinda had one brother (Alex), two years older. He was her sister's opposite. Alex had already pledged a fraternity, was drinking heavily, smoking grass, and failing two courses. "As normal as pie," his mother had said. Then, one day, Belinda stopped by Wal-Mart in the early afternoon. A robbery and shoot-out ensued that left the three robbers dead in the parking lot. Perhaps because she was young, attractive and had been in one of the check-out lines when the action started, Belinda was interviewed by three local TV stations and two cable networks. Her commentary was precise, natural, and flowed without any awkward pauses. She smiled and seemed as professional as her questioners. Belinda's parents were stunned by her performance. "Where did that come from?" her father inquired. When Belinda arrived back home, she appeared nonplussed by the many positive e-mails, Twitter comments and other social media posts from around the nation and even overseas. There were also non-stop telephone calls, including her high school principal Mrs. Lundgren. She asked if Belinda would agree to speak at a special all-school assembly in three days. "I think people would like to hear from you," the principal said. "O. K., I guess," Belinda had answered. After hanging up the phone, the teenager sat down with her parents and said with some trepidation: "What do I do now?" Her mother thought for a moment and from somewhere came an idea. "Why don't you go talk to Pastor Charles, the new interim minister at church? He is a nice man and a good Sunday speaker. He might have some ideas for you." For some reason, the suggestion appealed to Belinda. The new minister had a non-threatening shyness about him that seemed familiar to her. The next day, she called the church for an appointment. The Reverend picked up his own telephone and said, "Sure. I am really flattered, Belinda. I saw you on TV and thought you did a great job with the media. Come on over to the church this afternoon after school." When Belinda sat down in the school cafeteria at lunch, she was surrounded by many people who had never

John 14: 15-17

spoken to her before. It was a nice feeling, but a bit unreal. During her discussion later with Pastor Charles, he had said an interesting thing that resonated with her: "Belinda, each of us has the Holy Spirit of God living right here inside of us. When you are speaking at the school assembly, keep telling yourself: "It is not I, but the Holy Spirit within me that does the work." *I think you'll do fine." And she did. The assembly was covered by two local TV stations. Afterwards, one of the reporters told her, "Young lady, you have a great future in broadcasting. I think your college major just selected you. When you finish school, come see us about a job." And she did just that.*

JOHN 14: 18-20

JOHN 14: 18: I will not leave you as orphans; I will come to you.

JOHN 14: 19: Before long, the world will not see me anymore, but you will see me. Because I live, you will also live.

JOHN 14:20: On that day, you will realize that I am in the Father, and you are in me, and I am in you.

In John 14:18, Jesus keeps reassuring the Disciples that he will never abandon them. However, these men who had staked their lives and sacred honor on Jesus probably felt like orphans now that he was leaving them physically. Yet, the Master was proclaiming his ongoing presence and influence. Jesus did acknowledge that he would no longer be visible in a material sense. What did he really mean by the statement "Because I live, you will also live?" That sounded good, but what did it really mean? It suggested a dynamic that seemed unfamiliar and implausible. He was either dead or alive. How could there be a middle ground, somewhere between Heaven and the material world? Jesus also kept referring to a murky concept of "Oneness with God." How could he really be in the Father and the Father be in him? Didn't it have to be one or the other? Jesus often spoke the Disciples in hard to understand terms. But, after stunning them with the revelation of his departure, these esoteric explanations appeared vague and mysterious. The Disciples wanted to believe the Master was telling them. But he was not making it easy.

A Teacher's Legacy:

High school principal Veronica Lundgren was surprised when a district educational consultant recommended her for the Assistant Superintendent's job. She was not a bright young "comer" in any sense. Mrs. Lundgren had been a teacher and administrator for more than 30 years. Yes, she had always received plaudits and excellent reviews for her work with students, parents and fellow education professionals. In fact, there was not a single negative notation or comment in her personnel records. That was not an easy thing to achieve over a long career in the quicksand of school politics and parent interactions. Mrs. Lundgren had always been a "grinder" or "plodder". She opted for slow and steady gains in the learning process. Her long career was not "streaky" or unpredictable. Perhaps that steadiness was being more valued and rewarded now.

She had also been surprised four years ago when promoted to high school principal. However, her time in the job had been mostly without drama or controversy. For that, Veronica was grateful. With her husband Warren's recent cancer diagnosis and chemo treatments, she already had enough distractions. After being promoted to the assistant superintendent's position, but before she left the principal's job, Veronica received an interesting letter. It was signed by four former students of varying ages and visibility: They were "Maria", "Samantha", "Tremaine", and "Bobby". Mrs. Lundgren remembered all four to some degree. They were asking to meet with her before she left for the administrative job. Of course, she granted their request. A time was set in her office at the high school. When they arrived separately, Veronica was taken a little aback by their various ages. "Maria" was a fifth grader now and a fiery little Hispanic beauty. Mrs. Lundgren only had the little girl one year, when Maria had just arrived from Mexico with her mother Gabriella. There was some hesitancy by the school to accept Maria because of her immigration status, but Veronica liked both mother and daughter and stuck up for them. It made a difference. Gabriella had eventually married the son of an African American law enforcement officer and a female ER doctor. The young family seemed to be doing well. "Samantha" had been one of Mrs. Lundgren's favorites, for some reason. The little urchin had the foulest mouth of any third grader Veronica had ever experienced. Every other word began with either "fu-----g", "as-----le," or "b----h". She was always getting into fights with other girls and even a few smaller boys on occasion. Samantha was capable of bullying anybody. One day, Veronica had spent an hour talking to her about the anti-social behavior. "You're an attractive girl if you could lose the attitude," the teacher told her. She had also slung some profanity back at Samantha, a real risk. However, things had surprisingly improved after that encounter. The last thing Mrs. Lundgren remembered was

John 14: 18-20

attending a school play featuring Samantha. She was a big hit with the audience. The former potty mouth had found her niche. "Tremaine" was a much harder case. He had witnessed his older brother being murdered in the family front yard. His father was serving life in prison for a pair of killings. Those kinds of negative outcomes are not easily forgotten. Mrs. Lundgren had spent hours after school with Tremaine trying to help him sort his feelings. She was determined that this one young man would not be permanently scarred or give up hope. He was in high school now and a budding star on football team. There was even talk of a college scholarship with a Division I program. A former NFL star had supposedly taken an interest in the young man's future. Tremaine had come a long way indeed. The, there was "Bobby". Growing up, he was the poster child for juvenile delinquency. One fall afternoon. he and Veronica had been arguing after school. She had placed him in detention and the young boy started cursing her for it. The teacher walked back to his desk. Bobby suddenly stood up and struck her full in the face with his fist. Veronica's glasses spun off her head and she staggered backward. Bobby just stared at his surprised teacher with a look of absolute shock. "Oh, my God," he shouted, "I'm really sorry, Mrs. Lundgren." In that instant, Veronica realized she had a choice. She could run out of the room with her bruised cheek and shattered glasses and report Bobby's actions immediately to her principal and school security. It would mean an immediate suspension for the youngster and maybe a complete expulsion. She thought about her options. Then, a thought came from somewhere. "I'll forgive you," she told the repentant young man, "If you will come see me for one hour every day after school for a month. We will talk about life, your life. That is your punishment. Take it or leave it." Bobby took her offer with deep gratitude. Things had changed for him after that in ways he could not have imagined. He would be leaving for pre-law studies at an Ivy League school in the fall. Maria, Samantha,

Tremaine and Bobby trooped into their former teacher's office one by one. When everyone was seated, Mrs. Lundgren smiled and asked, "What can I do for you?" "You've already done it," they all answered in unison. And she had.

JOHN 14: 21-22

JOHN 14: 21—Whosever has my commands and keeps them is the one who loves me. The one who loves me will be loved by my Father, and I too will love them and show myself to them."

JOHN 14:22—Then Judas (not Judas Iscariot) says, "But Lord, why do you intend to show yourself to us and not the world?"

In John 14:21, Jesus seems to again focus on making sure the Christ teachings do not end with his departure. He specifically links the Disciples love for him to a continuing practice of his principles. If they will keep the "commands", that demonstrates their unswerving love and devotion. In turn, Jesus promises that their obedience will result in an affectionate response toward them from God. However, Jesus' unusual statement that he too will "love them and show himself to them" probably created ripples of confusion. Was he really leaving or not? How could he be gone physically, yet show himself to them? The uncertainty was immediately confirmed by the "other" Judas. He asked Jesus for clarification from Jesus about what the Disciples were being told. Their spiritual leader might be the Son of God and Messiah all rolled into one. But the Disciples were still bold enough to ask for specifics. In any case, these sudden events had probably unnerved the Master to some extent. As his departure loomed, Jesus was seeking to confirm that his sacred teachings (and God's holy words) would not depart with him.

The Forgotten Coach:

Angus McSwain was not surprised by the cancer. The 85-year old former high school football coach had almost expected its arrival. Angus had lost his beloved wife of 60 years, Miss Lillian, the year before. "The Old Scotchman", as he was often called back in his coaching days, knew that longtime marriage partners soon became ill and passed shortly after their spouses succumbed. So, the cancer diagnosis itself was not a surprise. Young Doc Redman had been gentle with the announcement. "It's pretty predictable," the doctor had said with a sympathetic frown. "It's your standard glioma", he said. "It's a tough form of brain cancer that usually runs itself out in about a year and a half. I wish I could offer you some hope, Mr. McSwain, but less than 5% of my patients survive any longer, I would respectfully suggest you think about geting things organized." Angus had grinned and said: "First of all, Doc, it's "Coach McSwain". I have been called that since I was 27 years old. I quit being a "Mister" a long time ago." "I meant no disrespect," Dr. Redman smiled, "Did you coach around here?" "Well, I have been gone from around here for a long time," Angus smiled. "I coached at the old high school. In fact, I saw the husband of the current high principal's husband in your office the last time I was here. Mr. Lundgren, I believe. He's caught the "Big C" too, I guess?" The young doctor shook his head and said: "You know I can't comment on other patients, Mr. (I mean) coach McSwain." Angus nodded and replied, "Well, it doesn't matter. Yes, I was the head coach up there for 20 years before they fired me. It did not seem to matter that I had won three state championships. You know, Doc, I had 18 winning seasons out of those 20 years. But when a female P. E. teacher accused me of leering at her, that was it. I was gone in a week. It did not seem right, but that's life these days. At least Miss Lillian stood by me. "That's too bad," the doctor offered. "What did you do after that?" Angus frowned, lowered his head briefly and then snapped it back before he answered. "Actually, nothing," he said. "I couldn't get a job coaching Pop Warner ball. I kicked around for a while and then started selling cars. Lots of folks remembered me from coaching and liked discussing football before buying an automobile. I was the Sales Manager for the Toyota dealership out there on the Interstate for more than 25 years before I retired. Many of my customers still called me "Coach McSwain." "Well, it sounds like you did OK after leaving the coaching profession," the young doc observed. "Yes, but I do have some regrets," Angus replied. "You've heard about "Shotgun" offense? I invented that one in high school. It helped us win a couple of state titles. I tried to convince my successor to keep it going, but he did not want to do anything to do with it.. How about the "45" defense with five linemakers? That was my idea too. The school dropped it the year after I was fired. They did not

John 14: 21-22

win a game the next season. The pros have been using a variation of it for many years. I was also the first coach that developed the tight end position. Two of my high school kids made good livings in the NFL off that idea." "It sounds like you had quite a career, Coach", the oncologist remarked. "Say, I would like to keep reminiscing. However, I do have a few other patients to see. Do you want to share anything else before we wrap up?" "Yes, I kind of do," the old coach concluded. "The next time you watch some football on TV or in person, think about me. There is a good chance you are seeing something that I invented 50 years ago. If one person remembers you, I guess it has been a good life. Right?" "I'll keep that in mind, Coach," the doc smiled as he stood in respect and shook the old man's hand, "I will definitely keep it in mind. You might be surprised at who else might remember you. One never knows whose life they might touch."

JOHN 14: 23-24

JOHN 14:23—Anyone who loves me will obey my teaching. My Father will love them, and we will come to them and make our home with them.

JOHN 14:24—Anyone who does not love me will not obey my teaching. These words you hear are not my own; they belong to the Father who sent me.

Jesus invokes his sacred alliance with God in pressuring the Disciples to continue obeying "my teaching". If they will keep the Christ doctrine in place, Jesus promises reciprocal love from both he and God. If his followers want to claim God's divine love as their own, maintaining Jesus' instructions stands as the key. The Master also presents the idea that his Holy words did not originate with him. They came directly from God, the Creator of the universe. So, should the Disciples choose not to carry his teachings forward, they would not only be failing him. They would be dishonoring God, in whose name Jesus was speaking. It might one thing to let their friend and leader down. But, to ignore God as the origination point for the Christ teachings would be something else indeed. There is no doubt that Jesus was pressing his points with The Disciples, still reeling from the stunning revelation about their LORD departing soon. Time was running short for the Master to nail down a commitment from his closest cohorts.

Helping Tremaine:

Former NFL tight end Brett Moran read Coach McSwain's recent obituary twice. Brett knew that his late father, a pro football tight end in his own right, had played for Angus McSwain in high school and loved the crusty coach. Brett smiled when he thought about his dad and the coach playing catch in Heaven. "He invented the tight end position," his father had told him about the legendary coach, "I would have been nothing without him." Brett had inherited many of his dad's football skills. However, he was much larger in height and weight, measuring six-foot five and weighing 255 pounds. Being a good blocker as well a dangerous runner after the catch helped Brett put together a nine-year NFL career with three different teams. He had even played for the winning team in a Super Bowl. His wife Judy made sure his heavy SB ring was always bright and shiny. Since retiring from his pro career, Brett had signed on as a talent scout for a major Division I university.

Without any expectations, he had stopped by one evening to watch a local high school football game. One of the players immediately caught his attention. It helped that the young man happened to play the tight end position. After the game, Brett sought out the budding star in the home team's locker room. The kid's name was Tremaine Robinson. Although shy, Brett learned that Tremaine had only taken up football recently. He was academically a senior, but only a first-year athlete and a walk-on at that. A high school assistant coach had seen Tremaine in a pickup neighborhood game with players of various age and skill levels. The youngster was better than anyone else by far. At first, Tremaine did not seem interested in going out for the high school team. "It is just too late for me to start now," he said. However, the assistant coach was persistent. From the first day of practice, the other coaches and the youngster's teammates were astonished by Tremaine's natural abilities. Soon after the season began, he moved into the starting line-up at tight end. During his first game, he caught a total of nine passes, including two for touchdowns. Suddenly, the unheralded youngster was drawing raves from everyone. People wanted to know more about him. He would not answer any questions about his background, just shaking his head and remaining silent. That naturally stirred up the press to begin digging for themselves. One local sports reporter soon discovered troubling facts about Tremaine's family and personal background. His older brother had been shot and killed in the family's front yard five years before. His father then proceeded to track down the two gang bangers responsible. He pumped three bullets into each one and was subsequently tried and convicted of murder. He was now serving two consecutive 50-year terms in the state prison. Tremaine himself got off track. He began hanging around with an older crowd that was always doing something illegal. Three of his "posse" had concocted a plan to stage a daylight robbery at a local Wal-Mart. It was an insane plan that ultimately resulted in a deadly shootout with a SWAT team. All three of his "friends" had lost their lives. They had initially recruited Tremaine to serve as a lookout during the robbery. At the last minute, the school principal (Mrs. Lundgren) had demanded his presence at a one-on-one meeting with her. If he failed to show, she promised to expel him. Things were beginning to jell with an assistant coach of the school football team, so Tremaine did not want to upset that possibility. Anyway, he kept the school appointment and missed the fatal shootout. When the negative publicity about his family hit in the paper, ex NFL tight end Brett called the young man to have lunch. When Tremaine arrived at the fast food restaurant, he found someone else with Brett. It was the head coach of a nationally ranked Division I football program. "Let me be the first to offer you a full football scholarship next fall," the coach had said, "But I am certain that I won't be the last."

JOHN 14:25-26

JOHN 14: 25—All this I have spoken while still with you.

JOHN 14: 26—But the Advocate, the Holy Spirit, whom the Father will send in my name, will teach you all things and will remind you of everything I have said to you.

The spiritual concept of The Holy Spirit as a comforter and "Advocate" confirms our human connection to God. We are being advised that our Creator has installed a link with the divine at our very core. As such, the Holy Spirit also promises to perform the work that God assigns to us. We can step aside and watch in amazement as this inner force goes about its supernatural business. In this revelation, Jesus is explaining that a part of him will always be present within the Disciples. God will be sending the Holy Spirit as a fitting and permanent replacement. It will not only serve as a teacher and inspirer, but also a fellow worker in the spiritual vineyard. Both God and Jesus are asking the Disciples to trust and accept this invisible force. Without question, it is a "Big Ask". Jesus' closest followers are a practical and even simple group. Being able to accept the implausible idea of an invisible "Holy Spirit" will require the highest level of trust and devotion.

The Daughter:

Charlene had been a nursing supervisor at the American Clinic in Tokyo for four years when the virus blew in from China. Things had gone well for Char since she left the U. S. Her marriage to Kristin, a tech executive for a California company, was thriving. Charlene had adapted well to the pace and purpose of Japanese life. The gentleness of the people combined surprisingly well with their practical and industrious lifestyle. She did not miss the random violence and sometimes crudeness of her native country. Charlene did miss rooting for the Green Bay Packers. Sometimes Char wondered if perhaps she had been Japanese in another life. Everything seemed so familiar to her. Would she ever return to the U. S., even for a visit? Her mother Linda had passed soon after the move to Japan. She had felt a bit guilty about not flying home to comfort Charles, her widowed minister dad. But she had never really been close to either of her parents. Her life in Tokyo kept her more than occupied. The medical personnel at the Clinic were a friendly and family-like group. Then, without warning, the virus sidled in quietly. Within a month, it was an inferno of pain and misery. People began dying, first by the dozens, then by the hundreds and finally by the thousands. The Clinic was overrun with patients. Many were Americans who had formerly lived in the states. A huge number were retired members of the U. S. military, married to Japanese women. Charlene was amazed how many patients would arrive at the clinic with mild symptoms and then be dead in less than a week. So many ex-military people had underlying symptoms, which contributed to their quick demise from the virus. She had never smoked, but the plague seemed to specialize in destroying already compromised respiratory systems. Her hours at the clinic began expanding. Soon, she was experiencing a high level of stress. Her usually positive relationship with Kristin began fraying. There was no way that anyone would ever understand how living with death could be so negative. Charlene then tested positive for the virus and entered quarantine. Her dreams soon took on nightmarish qualities. At midnight one evening she slipped into a dream state that rattled her. In the dream, Charlene had died. She arrived alone at the gates of Heaven. She had always heard that when you passed, you would be greeted by a throng of people from your past. Char looked hard for a welcoming committee. However, she only saw two figures peering out from behind the pearly gates. One she immediately recognized as her mother. Linda stood with folded arms and a non-committal expression on her face. The other form was a scraggly looking woman with unkempt hair. She had a cigarette dangling from her mouth. Charlene edged closer to get a better look at the old lady, but nothing registered. The woman removed the cigarette and said "Well, you finally got here. It is about time. Now we might get to spend time together, unless of course you have other plans." She seemed almost angry and perplexed. "Who are you?" Charlene asked. "I'm your Holy

John 14: 25-26

Spirit, honey," the lady said with a frown. *"You never once asked me to do anything for you. You did not listen to God either, for the most part. The pandemic finally did get your attention. The Father had a lot of plans for you, but you never listened to any voice besides your own. Look how you treated this nice woman right here, your mother. And do not get me started about the nasty treatment of your dad. He has a wonderful reputation up here already. Pastor Charles is such a caring man. But then, you never paid much attention to either your mom or your dad. When was the last time that you called him? Oh, forget it! I am sure you do not even remember! Do you even have his new address?" "Hey, wait a minute,"* Charlene said, *"I thought everything in Heaven was positive. I do not care for the way you are grilling me. What do you think about it, mother. Is this standard procedure for the way people get welcomed to Heaven? If this is it, I may just choose to stay back on earth."* Her mother just smiled and said, *"If you do go back, please call your father. He is still hoping to hear from you. Charles will be joining me here in Heaven in just three short years. But I know that time would be happier if he heard something from you. We both loved you, Charlene. But Charles had a "Father's Love" for you. He never stopped believing in you, even when you ignored us. Remember, it was he and I (plus God) that created you in the first place. To Charles, however, you were always his beautiful little girl. Now, you must go back and get well. We cannot have you arriving up here before your father. He wouldn't be able to get over it."* Then, the present time returned and uprooted Charlene's consciousness. She laid in her bed for a few minutes and then hit the nurse's call button. *"Could you please fetch me my cell phone?"* she asked the night nurse. *"I need to call my dad."*

JOHN 14: 27

JOHN 14:27—Peace I leave with you; my peace I give you. I do not give to you as the world gives. Do not let your hearts be troubled and do not be afraid.

John 14: 27

Although the NIV edition of the Bible does not include the phrase: "I give you the peace that surpasses all understanding", many other interpretations do. Jesus knows the Disciples are not at peace. How could they be? Their Messiah is leaving them. These loyal followers of Jesus are uncertain about both the present and the future. Attaining any kind of "Peace" appears impossible for them right now. Anxiety is rampant. Personal uncertainty rules the day. How often in our own human lives do we long for the "Peace" that Jesus promises? It is a deep peacefulness that eludes us in a troubled world. We live in a roiled culture where unrest now outranks peace. Yet, there is something in most every human heart that values and seeks peace. Again, Jesus understood the need for his Disciples to find some sort of peace amidst the chaos. They would be unable to continue his ministry while living in an unpeaceful environment. Jesus is asking for courage, and trust at a time of maximum upset. Of course, their hearts were troubled. Absolutely, they were afraid. What could restore the Disciples to peace? Maybe this promise of peace from Jesus himself might help.

Samantha's Talents:

Teenage Samantha could out swear any man, boy or sailor. No other female potty mouth came close to her profane outbursts. Where did this dubious talent originate? Her 100% dysfunctional family probably would claim most of the credit, if you could call it that. There were four immediate members of the Cromwell family. Her brother Thaddeus (He preferred "Tha-do") was nineteen and two years older than Sam. He played bass in his own rock group (The Tricksters). The band was already in its sixth incarnation in three years. Samantha's father was known as "A. William Cromwell" in his mid-size downtown law firm. To his out-of-control daughter, dad was "A. Perfect A------e". She often referred to him as such, even at rare family dinners. But it was Samantha's mother that she dueled with most often. Nancy Cromwell was an afternoon Vodka drinker. Two other neighbor ladies usually showed up around 3 p.m. for daily commiserations about husbands and assorted teenagers. The alcohol laced therapy session usually ended around 5 p.m. The wives were expected at home then for cocktail hour with their respective husbands. Samantha tried to arrive home by 5:30 p.m. so that she and the folks could poke at each other for a while before everyone went their own way for dinner. Sam usually adjourned to the bedroom to spend some time with her latest passion: pot. She had become a marijuana gourmet. She tried to sample a different product every week and then report her assessment to friends. Her biggest impediment to happiness these days was that stick-in-the-mud Mrs. Lundgren. The high school principal had been on her lately about the swearing. Sam had told off the chemistry teacher Mr. O'Shaughnessy one day after he had given her an "F+" on a paper about the element AU (Gold). "You don't know s--- about anything, you m----------r." she had shouted at him. "Mr. O", a former Army Green Beret had heard the term directed at him in many languages. He had briefly considered chopping the unruly student in her carotid artery with the edge of his hand. He pulled back at the last minute. Instead, he wrote her up with the high school principal. Mrs. Lundgren summoned the teenager to her office the following day. "Sit down, you stupid b----," the principal yelled at her. "No, stand up!" the old lady instructed her. Samantha was confused. No adult had ever confronted her with such ferocity. "Face the wall, m--------r" the principal shouted. Sam could not believe she was being talked to in this fashion. She pulled out her cell phone to record the principal's rage. It would be a juicy download on Instagram after school tonight. She might even share it with her mother and the Vodka Sisters. Maybe Nancy would get steamed up at Mrs. Lundgren's actions and let her off the hook for a while. "Are you high again, wench?" Mrs. Lundgren said, dripping with sarcasm. Now, the *principal was really hitting close to home. Sam tried to keep her pot use somewhat undercover. However, without a doubt, she had been high in Spanish Immersion class the other day. Just for giggles, she began speaking in Italian. Mr. Hernandez, the Spanish teacher, had not been amused. He made her stay after school and conjugate Spanish verbs for two hours. At the end of that torture and while she was still stoned, he had left her alone in the classroom. Now, the principal was shouting at her. "Put your skinny butt in that chair, Missy," Mrs. L said. The principal then handed Sam a piece of paper, while saying "Now first sign this and then I will let you read it." She thrust a pen into the teenager's hand. "What the hell?" Samantha said, but scribbled her name on the typed sheet of paper. Mrs. Lundgren then pulled up a chair less than a foot from the girl's face. "Now, I will tell you what you just signed," she said. "You just joined Mrs. Franz's drama group. She is doing auditions for a play this afternoon. It is about a dysfunctional family that swears a lot. You should feel right at home. If fact, I suggested you for the role of the potty-mouth teenaged daughter. I think you would be perfect. You have a great little actress inside of you, Samantha. It is past time you took advantage of that talent. Now, shoo! I have work to do. Take this piece of paper and give it to Mrs. Franz. You do not need to let me know whether you got the part. I have it on good authority that you are a lock. However, reserve me a ticket for opening night. I like the front row. I will be right there, cheering you on. Don't disappoint me, you hear."*

JOHN 14: 28-31

John 14: 28—You heard me say, "I am going away and I am coming back to you. If you loved me, you would be glad that I am going to the Father, for the Father is greater than I.

John 14: 29—I have told you now before it happens, so that when it does happen you will believe.

John 14:30—I will not say much more to you, for the prince of the world is coming, He has no hold over me.

John 14:31—but he comes so that the world may learn that I love my Father and do exactly what my Father has commanded me. Come now, let us leave."

John 14: 28-31

There is deep meaning in the final four verses of John 14. Jesus wants the Disciples to accept his coming departure. He is also holding out hope to them that he will someday return. Jesus wants his followers to understand his happiness. He is indeed going to be with a greater spiritual Deity than himself. The Master has informed the Disciples only in general terms about the coming days. They could hardly imagine the physical and emotional trauma that awaits him. He offers them no preview of either the Crucifixion or Resurrection. He could have even felt some of their uncertainty. Yet, he still assures the Disciples that the "princes" of the material world will never exert any hold over him. This suggests that Jesus may have some inkling about the coming miracle of the Resurrection. The Master promises that the world will someday realize the extent of his love for God and absolute obedience to the Father's plan for his spiritual destiny.

Bobby:

When he turned 13, Bobby became an uncontrollable troublemaker. Sometimes it seemed that a malevolent dark power was manipulating his strings like a wooden puppet. He honestly did not understand where some of his evil ideas and actions originated. Bobby even imagined that he might be serving as some kind human channel through which evil flowed. His first official arrest came at 14. He was apprehended by a black police officer named Paul after running over a senior citizen with a bicycle. It did not help that he had stolen the bike, increasing his exposure to the juvenile justice system. Besides the robbery and assault, injuring an 80-year old man added "Elder Abuse" to his legal jeopardy. The cop who had been arrested him seemed reasonably calm about the situation. However, the young teenager realized he was in real trouble. Both of his distraught parents arrived at the police station, each loudly blaming the other. It did not help that Bobby demonstrated a disrespectful "attitude" toward his mom and dad. Paul, the arresting officer, detected Bobby flashing them the middle finger. After it occurred for the second time, the policeman asked Bobby to accompany him to another office at the station. Paul then disappeared for a few minutes. When he returned there was another younger cop with him. "This is Troy," Paul introduced the officer. He was a tough guy too about 10 years ago. Then, he got smart. I am putting you in his custody for a few hours. Rather than sit in a jail cell waiting for a judge, this will be time better spent." Then, Paul left the room to visit with Bobby's parents. The teenager did not see him again that day. "Troy" did a short version of "Scared Straight" with Bobby, but it seemed to have no noticeable effect. The next day, a juvenile judge gave Bobby a stern lecture, but let him off with a warning. The youngster was helped when the 80-something victim, a former high school football coach named McSwain, declined to press charges. It was about a month later when the incident happened with his principal, Mrs. Lundgren. Hitting her with his fist so soon after the robbery/assault incident could have been a fatal combination for the teenager. For the first time, Bobby seemed to realize his vulnerability. He began cleaning up his act. The summer he turned 16, Mrs. Lundgren's husband helped Bobby land a minor job as an assistant lifeguard at a small private lake. One day when was working alone, while the head lifeguard was at lunch, Bobby saw a young girl in some distress about 50 yards from shore. Swimming was one of his athletic gifts. He did not hesitate racing into the water and bringing the girl back to dry land. The girl's mother, a nice Hispanic lady, was extremely grateful. She thanked Bobby profusely. "Maria could have drowned had you not been here," the woman told him. "My husband is a police officer and I just called him. He wanted to come over and thank you himself." When the officer arrived, Bobby and the cop looked at each other with instant recognition. "Is that you?" Paul inquired with some surprise. "Yes, it is," Bobby

John 14: 28-31

answered, "I didn't expect to see you again." Paul smiled and replied, *"I am glad you did, young man. I am certainly glad you did."*

THE TWELVE GIFTS OF JOHN 14

GIFT #1—HOPE
GIFT #2—TRUST
GIFT #3—ACCEPTANCE
GIFT #4—ONENESS
GIFT #5—THE HOLY SPIRIT
GIFT #6—PEACE
GIFT #7—SPIRITUAL SERVICE
GIFT #8—OBEDIENCE
GIFT #9—STRENGTH
GIFT #10--ENCOURAGEMENT
GIFT #11--COMFORT
GIFT #12—FAITH

The Gifts

GIFT #1—HOPE:
The Disciples were stunned by Jesus' announcement. It was almost impossible to process. Their leader, the Messiah, was leaving. He would be going away just a few days, weeks or even months. He had promised to come back for them at some point. But that seemed like a vague possibility. In any time of sudden loss, hope can be the first casualty. Life often blindsides us without warning. After our initial shock, reality begins to emerge. We start to understand the temporary and fragile nature of human life. But where do we find the hope required to keep going after the loss? Throughout John 14, Jesus tries to offer hope in many forms—The Holy Spirit being the most obvious. He is promising "Peace" beyond what the world can offer. The Master tells the Disciples they can do the Greater Works. He urges them not to worry or be afraid. He reassures them about the nature of God and extends the gift of Hope. He instructs the Disciples to accept this gift at their most forlorn moment. In our own time of loss and uncertainty, we too can find comfort and hope in the promises of God. *Read Romans 15: 13, Deuteronomy 31:6, Psalm 39:7, Jeremiah 29:11, Proverbs 23:18, John 11:18, Ephesians 1:18.*

GIFT #2—TRUST:
The spiritual life requires that we trust the invisible over the visible. Trusting the unseen often can seem "blind" and impractical to anyone immersed in the material world. If you are unable to see it, hear it, touch it, taste it or smell it, it remains hard to accept something as real. Trusting an invisible God can seem most daunting. To the Disciples, Jesus was real because they could experience Him with their five senses. Now that human connection would soon disappear, perhaps forever. Continuing to trust the unseen could demand a much higher level of devotion. Jesus seemed

to understand this might be a problem for His followers. When we get confronted with a loss, it is tempting to put ourselves in control of the response. Many of us are taught that we must be responsible for controlling our own destiny. Putting that personal control aside and turning things over to a Higher Power can seem impossible. Yet, in trusting something beyond ourselves, we can often find the best answer to dealing with personal crises. ***Read Jeremiah 17:7-8, Proverbs 3: 5-6, Psalms 91:1-2, Isaiah 43:2, 2 Corinthians 5:7, Hebrews 13:6, Philippians 4:19, 1 John 4:16***

GIFT #3—ACCEPTANCE

Jesus was himself in the throes of an "acceptance" crisis. He was not only urging the Disciples to accept a new reality. After an incredible three-year ministry of miracles and accomplishment, God was summoning His only son home to Heaven. Before Jesus would arrive in The Kingdom, he would face a human trial, the unthinkable pain of Crucifixion and a triumphant Resurrection. What a rollercoaster of emotions! Then, besides the personal and emotional challenges, The Master must convince his followers to accept what might be coming. Acceptance in spiritual terms does not mean total failure or abject surrender. It means finding clarity in all things. It represents coming to terms with an unforeseen human situation from a spiritual standpoint. Would the Disciples accept their own fate, whatever it might be? ***Read 1 Peter 3:9, John 3:16, Romans 8:31, Matthew 5: 38-42 Colossians 3: 12, John 1:12, 2 Corinthians 5:17.***

GIFT #4—ONENESS

The Holy Trinity represents one of the greatest spiritual concepts ever revealed. The terms Father (God), Son (the Christ) and the Holy Spirit are not three separate things. Instead, they represent three different aspects of the one God. As human beings, merging ourselves into oneness with God and the Spirit within, we can more fully deal with a chaotic world. We meet the twists and turns of material life with a unique trio of spiritual resources. If we are wise, The concept of the Holy Trinity will always be incorporated into our basic approach to life. Becoming one with God and the Holy Spirit that lives within each of us offers the best plan for overcoming the world. *Read Colossians 1:19, John 10:30, Revelation 1:8, Ephesians 4:6, Isaiah 43:10, John 14:9-11, Matthew 10: 20.*

GIFT #5—THE HOLY SPIRIT

Many knowledgeable voices state that the Holy Spirit within us performs the work God requires. "It is not I, but the Christ within that does the work," brings a promise of spiritual success that human beings cannot hope to duplicate. In that sense, we are blessed that God created us with the gift of the inner Christ. No matter how daunting the chore may be, we never need face any task alone. In John 14, Jesus also refers to The Holy Spirit as "The Advocate". It is no small advantage having God forever based at the core of our being. We all can use a permanent "Advocate," considering how fickle and unfair the world can sometimes be. The Holy Spirit always remains "on call" and prepared to stand up on our behalf whenever needed. We are always helped and supported by the Spirit of God in our midst. *Read 1 Corinthians 6:19, Isaiah 11:2, Acts 1:8, John 16: 12-15, Ezekiel 36:26-27, Romans 8:9, Matthew 10:20.*

GIFT #6—PEACE

In John 14, this was not a time of "Peace" for Jesus or His surprised Disciples. Everything was suddenly turning uncertain. Our own peacefulness can likewise be ripped away by an unexpected event or situation. We all crave peace and stability. Few human beings enjoy change in any form. While "still" waters' soothe the spirit, churning and angry waters bring fear and unrest. When storms come, our best source of peace lies in a close relationship with God.

John 14

You can sense Jesus aligning Himself ever closer to the Father. Whatever was coming, and evidence suggests that Jesus knew His fate, being closer to God stands as the wisest decision. If they would follow His lead, the Master promised the "peace that surpasses understanding." When our world becomes upset, we also can find peace in that same assurance. ***Read John 16:33, 2 Thessalonians 3:16, Isaiah 26:3, Philippians 4:6-7, Romans 15:13, Psalm 4:8, Jude 1:2, Job 22:21.***

GIFT #7—SPIRITUAL SERVICE
During Jesus' remarks at the Last Supper, He kept reminding the Disciples of their spiritual mission. He tells them to "keep his commands". Jesus also assures His followers they can do the greater works. He realizes that the Disciples must believe in themselves. This will be more difficult without His inspirational leadership. In so many words, Jesus urges them to focus on spiritual service. When we get confused about what to do after an unexpected upset, concentrating on serving God offers the best plan. Keeping our thoughts and actions centered on the spiritual provides the best path forward. God needs our hands, our feet, and our actions to accomplish spiritual objectives. We need to stay focused on Spirit in the most difficult moments. In human life, hard times are guaranteed. Being of service to God can help get us through anything. ***Read 2 Corinthians 9-12, Ephesians 4:12, 1 Peter 4:9-11, Galatians 5:13, Colossians 3: 23-24, Romans 12: 11, 1 Samuel 12:24.***

GIFT #8—OBEDIENCE
Being spiritually obedient can be a challenge for human beings. People seek control in most every area of their lives. To be obedient requires humility and surrender. Getting the ego to stand aside for any reason is never easy. It struggles against shifting the focus away from its ongoing need for attention. Agreeing to obey God often feels

unnatural. It takes supreme trust and belief in a Higher Power. The human element in us wants to debate and argue with God. Spirit sometimes must remind us: we possess free will choice. God allows us to choose our own path. ***Read Isaiah 1:19, Philippians 2:8, Luke 11:28, Exodus 19:5, Romans 8:28, Hebrews 5:9, Deuteronomy 28:1.***

GIFT #9—STRENGTH

The events revealed in John 14 show the need for spiritual strength. The mental and emotional endurance of both Jesus and His Disciples is being severely tested. One can only imagine how Jesus must have felt, knowing what lay ahead for Him. But the Disciples also required strength as well. They were facing deep uncertainty about the future, including the issue of personal safety. Were they worried? The three denials of Peter, foretold by Jesus, demonstrate personal fear and concern. The days ahead would be perplexing and worrisome for all of Jesus' followers. When things become doubtful, God offers us the necessary strength to survive. All we need to do is ask and receive. Spirit possesses enough awesome strength for every type of situation. ***Read Psalm 46: 1-3, Nehemiah 8:10, 1 Chronicles 16:11, Deuteronomy 31:8, Isaiah 43: 1-3, Philippians 4-6, Joshua 1:9.***

GIFT #10—ENCOURAGEMENT

Jesus understood the human need of the Disciples for encouragement. They had given up their lives and fortunes to follow the Messiah. He was the Lord whom they faithfully served. There was no doubt the Disciples felt inadequate to take his place. These were the biggest shoes in the world to fill. How often do we feel unworthy and not prepared to meet someone's expectations? With God's help, we can also accomplish great things. Jesus was encouraging His followers by reminding them of God's total devotion. The Father would never leave them hopeless and abandoned under any circumstance. In His own way, Jesus

John 14

was also promising "I will never leave you or forsake you." Despite the physical scene, He would still be encouraging them. Some of the most reassuring words in John 14 come when Jesus tells the Disciples they will do "The Greater Works." How could that be possible? Would they be performing miracles, healing the sick and taking away blindness? The Master seemed to be saying they would indeed be doing those things and more. That was the ultimate encouragement for anyone. ***Read Zephaniah 3:17, Matthew 6:34, Psalm 55:22, 2 Corinthians 4: 16-18, Isaiah 26:3, Deuteronomy 31:8, 1 Chronicles 16:11.***

GIFT #11—COMFORT

There is no question Jesus was seeking to comfort The Disciples with His kind and loving words in John 14. He knew they were grieving his coming departure. Every individual must deal with grief in his and her own way. Sudden and unanticipated losses can be even harder. That type of grief can often be disorientating. It can take more time to process. One minute, a spouse or significant other, child, grandparent, other relative, friend, neighbor or business associate may be present in our lives. Then without warning, the connection is severed forever. Although Jesus had told The Disciples that they would soon "see Me no more", it still not make sense to them. Our human minds require extra time to process major shifts. Nobody is 100% able to understand and react with perfect comprehension when an unexpected loss whipsaws us. Jesus could only imagine the shock permeating The Disciples minds. He wants to offer them comfort and assurance. God is always ready to comfort us in our time of grief and loss, no matter how sudden or expected. We need to accept Spirit's offer to help. It can make a difference. ***Read 2 Corinthians 1-4, Psalm 23:4, Matthew 11:28-30, Isaiah 49:13, Romans 8:26-28, John 16:22, Revelation 21:4.***

GIFT #12—FAITH

No matter what problems we face in the material world, everything is made better with faith in God. For the faithless or those wavering in faith, the emotional journey can prove more daunting. As Jesus faced an imminent arrest, trial and Crucifixion, faith must have seemed all that remained. Jumping ahead to the blessed Sunday morning of Resurrection would have required mountains of faith on every believer's part. When we are in the middle of chaos or turmoil, it is not an easy thing to stop, think and regroup. But if we take the time to locate our faith factor, negative thoughts can begin to diminish. They lose their power to create or further inflame paralyzing fear. In John 14, every word from Jesus seems to ask for faith from the Disciples. Many of the His comments were aimed at activating their faith during a time of ultimate crisis. Jesus wanted to appeal to the "believer" in every Disciple, (except for Judas the betrayer). He knew that the power of faith would eventually dictate the future for His ministry. ***Read Hebrews 11:1, John 11:40, Psalm 46:10, Matthew 17:20, Ephesians 3:16-17, Galatians 2:16, 2 Corinthians 5-7.***

CONCLUSION

Conclusion

Thank you for taking the time to consider the many gifts of John 14. Without question, this chapter is crucial in the history of Christianity. The farewell discourse of Jesus at the Last Supper offers comfort to His followers. The revelation about The Holy Spirit illustrates the mystical connection between God and humanity. Jesus tells the Disciples they can accomplish the "Greater Works", thus encouraging the continuation of His ministry. Understanding their upset by His sudden departure, Jesus promises to leave them with a peace stronger than what the world can provide. The Master also expands on the concept of our divine Oneness with God. As we move forward in a chaotic world, I believe we can find hope and healing in the reassuring words of John 14. The Bible is our best spiritual guide to achieving a fulfilling human existence. May God bless and keep you on your own sacred journey. Know that you are loved.

ABOUT THE AUTHOR

Rev. Allen C. Liles is a graduate of Baylor University in Waco, TX and the Unity School of Religious Studies located at Unity Village, MO. Before being ordained as a nondenominational minister in 1993, he served as vice-president of public relations for The Southland Corporation (7-Eleven) in Dallas, TX and communications manager for The McLane Company in Temple, TX. Rev. Liles was also Senior Director of Outreach at Unity from 1995-2001, as well as serving Unity churches as a senior minister in Missouri, Arizona and Minnesota.

BOOKS by Allen C. Liles
Oh Thank Heaven! The Story of The Southland Corporation
Sitting With God/Meditating for God's Divine Guidance
The Forever Penny/How Our Loved Ones Stay Connected After Death
The 7 Puzzles of Life/God's Plan to Save the World

E-books on Smashwords.com
The 12 Promises of Heaven
Friends of Jesus
E-Spiritual Rehab
The Book of Celeste/God Recruits a Blogger to Save The World
The Book of Floyd/God Transforms a Racist
The Book of Ethan/God Confronts Teen Suicide

On AUDIBLE:
The Peaceful Driver/ Steering Clear of Road Rage

www.ingramcontent.com/pod-product-compliance
Lightning Source LLC
Chambersburg PA
CBHW072041110526
44592CB00012B/1510